Never Satisfied

NEVER SATISFIED

Story and pictures by
Fulvio Testa

HARCOURT BRACE & COMPANY
Orlando Atlanta Austin Boston San Francisco Chicago Dallas New York
Toronto London

"It's so boring here! Nothing exciting ever happens."

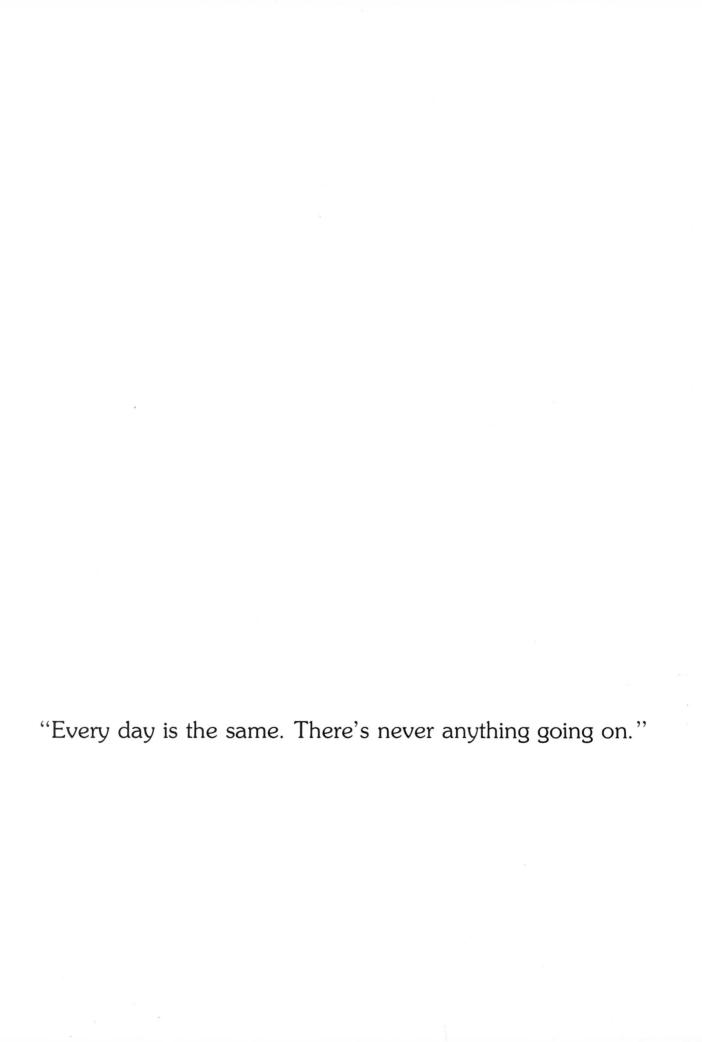

"Every day is the same. There's never anything going on."

"You always see the same old faces."

"No one ever does anything different."

"You're right. It's really boring here. I'd much rather live in the Amazon jungle…

...where there are *enormous* snakes."

"And wild panthers!"

"But I'm a panther."
"I said *wild* panthers."

"Oh, if only we were in the Amazon, with all those wild animals...

…and always in danger. We'd have such great adventures."

"It's no use wishing. We're stuck living here...

…where nothing exciting ever happens."

This edition is published by special arrangement with North-South Books Inc.

Grateful acknowledgment is made to North-South Books Inc., New York,
for permission to reprint *Never Satisfied* by Fulvio Testa. Copyright © 1982
by Nord-Süd Verlag AG; translation copyright © 1988 by North-South Books
Inc. Originally published in Switzerland under the title *Ein ganz
gewöhnlicher Tag*.

Printed in the United States of America

ISBN 0-15-302112-8

4 5 6 7 8 9 10   035   97 96 95